The month of March, from the illuminated manuscript *Les Trés Riches Heures du duc de Berry*

The Story of a Special Day
Volume 91

March

31

90th day of the year
(91st in leap years)
275 days remaining
until the end of the year.

by Michael Dobson

Timespinner
Press

Table of Contents

Cover: Detail from "Pont des Invalides et Tour Eiffel" (Photo: Carlos Delgado) — for the Event of the Day.

Jesse Owens

March 31 Quotations

"The battles that count aren't the ones for gold medals. The struggles within yourself — the invisible, inevitable battles inside all of us — that's where it's at."

— Jesse Owens, Olympic champion, died March 31, 1980

"One of the truly bad things about our politics is that it incites each administration to attack every last thing its predecessor has done, and to either tear down what was left or rename it so that its parentage can be forgotten."

— Al Gore, US Vice President and presidential candidate, born March 31, 1948

"Tell me how you measure me, and I will tell you how I behave."

— Eliyahu M. Goldratt, business theorist, born March 31, 1947

"I have this theory about words: There's a thousand ways to say, 'Pass the salt.' It could mean, you know, 'Can I have some salt?' or it could mean, 'I love you.' It could mean 'I'm very annoyed with you' — really, the list could go on and on. Words are little bombs, and they have a lot of energy inside them."

— Christopher Walken, actor, born March 31, 1943

"In a free society a large degree of human activity is none of the government's business. We should make criminal what's going to hurt other people and other than that we should leave it to people to make their own choices."

> — *Barney Frank, Massachusetts congressman,*
> *born March 31, 1940*

"*¡Sí se puede!*" ("It can be done!")

> — *César Chávez, labor organizer and social activist,*
> *born March 31, 1927. Personal motto, adopted as the*
> *official slogan of the United Farm Workers.*

"It is when we ask for love less and begin giving it more that the basis of human love is revealed to us."

> — *Leo Buscaglia, educator and writer,*
> *born March 31, 1924*

"It will fluctuate."

> — *J. P. Morgan, financier, died March 31, 1913, when*
> *asked "What will the stock market do?"*

"I can be on guard against my enemies, but God deliver me from my friends!"

— *Charlotte Brontë, novelist, died March 31, 1855*

"It is no use to blame the looking glass if your face is awry."

> — *Nikolai Gogol, novelist,*
> *born March 31 [O.S. March 19] 1809*

"Any man's death diminishes me, for I am involved in Mankind; and therefore never send to know for whom the bell tolls; it tolls for thee."

— *John Donne, poet, died March 31, 1631*

"But at my back I always hear / Time's winged chariot hurrying near; / And yonder all before us lie / Deserts of vast eternity."

— *Andrew Marvell, poet, born March 31, 1621,*
from "To His Coy Mistress."

Caricature of Gustave Eiffel (1887), Albert de Cours-Apres

Event of the Day

Eiffel Tower Opens

March 31, 1889, marked the opening of the Eiffel Tower. Originally designed as the entrance arch for the 1889 *Exposition Universelle* (World's Fair), and scheduled to last only twenty years, the Eiffel Tower has become one of the world's most recognizeable structures and the most visited paid monument in the world. Over 250 million people have ascended the Tower, nearly seven million in 2011 alone.

The tallest structure in Paris, the Eiffel Tower is 1,063 feet (324 meters) tall, roughly the same height as an 81-story building. At the time of its construction, it was the tallest man-made structure in the world, beating out the Washington Monument, which had earned the title the year before, and would hold the record until New York City's Chrysler Building opened in 1930. (In 1957, an antenna was added to the Eiffel Tower, and now it's 17 feet (5.2 meters) taller than its erstwhile rival.)

The tower is named for Gustave Eiffel, whose *Compagnie des Établissements Eiffel* designed and built the structure. As an engineer and construction executive, Eiffel had managed numerous projects, including bridges, viaducts, train stations, locomotives, and exhibition halls.

His first experience with monuments came in 1881, when sculptor Auguste Bartholdi hired Eiffel for his project to build the Statue of Liberty.

An expert in wind stresses, Eiffel designed the interior structure and pylon, and oversaw construction of the entire project until it was shipped to the United States.

The story of the Eiffel Tower begins in May 1884, as planning for the 1889 *Exposition Universelle* got underway. France had chosen 1889 as the year to host a World's Fair because it was the centennial of the storming of the Bastille in 1789, the beginning of the French Revolution. It was to be a mammoth show, covering nearly a square kilometer including the Champs de Mars, the Trocadéro, the quai d'Orsay, part of the Seine, and the Invalides esplanade. The fair would include a reconstruction of the Bastille, a hall for machinery that would be the longest interior space in the world at the time, and exhibitions from around the world. The United States offered a Wild West show featuring Buffalo Bill and Annie Oakley. The major attraction was a human zoo, the *Village négre*, with 400 Africans in "native" conditions.

Such an exhibition required a very special symbol, and in May 1884, senior Eiffel Company engineers Maurice Koechlin and Émile Nouguier came up with a radical concept: "a great pylon, consisting of four lattice girders standing apart at the base and coming together at the top, joined together by metal trusses at regular intervals." Although Eiffel initially was not enthusiastic about the project, he allowed his engineers to develop the concept and asked architect Stephen Sauvestre to add decoration and embellishment to the rather plain original design.

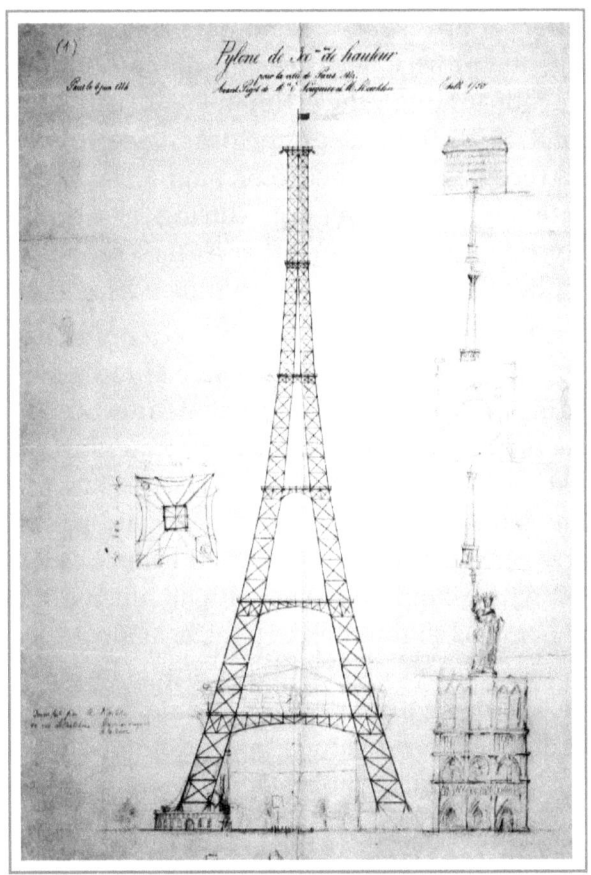

Original concept drawing of the Eiffel Tower by Maurice Koechlin.
Note the Statue of Liberty shown to scale.

The revised concept earned Eiffel's support, and he personally purchased the patent rights to the design. In 1886, a design competition selected his design as the centerpiece for the exposition. (The competition was rigged: all entries had to include a 300m four-sided metal tower, making Eiffel's design the only one that was fully worked out.)

Eiffel set up a separate, personal company to manage the project, and received 1.5 million francs for the job, although the estimated cost was about 6.5 million francs. To make up the difference, Eiffel would receive all income from commercial exploitation of the tower both during the exhibition and for twenty years thereafter. At the end of twenty years, the plan was for the tower to be demolished.

The Eiffel Tower was the subject of immediate controversy. A "Committee of Three Hundred," including a number of influential architects and members of the art community, came out strongly against the Tower. Their petition read in part: ""We, writers, painters, sculptors, architects and passionate devotees of the hitherto untouched beauty of Paris, protest with all our strength, with all our indignation in the name of slighted French taste, against the erection...of this useless and monstrous Eiffel Tower...To bring our arguments home, imagine for a moment a giddy, ridiculous tower dominating Paris like a gigantic black smokestack, crushing under its barbaric bulk Notre Dame, the Tour Saint-Jacques, the Louvre, the Dome of les Invalides, the Arc de Triomphe, all of our humiliated monuments will disappear in this ghastly dream. And for twenty years...we shall see stretching like a blot of ink the hateful shadow of the hateful column of bolted sheet metal..." Some of the protestors changed their minds when the tower was completed; others did not. French author Guy de Maupassant is supposed to have eaten lunch in the tower restaurant every day because it was the one place in Paris where he couldn't see the tower. However, today the Eiffel

Tower is considered one of the most beautiful and striking symbols of the city of Paris.

Construction of the tower began in January 1887 with the digging of foundations, and six months later the first of 18,038 pieces of metalwork began arriving on the construction site. Each piece was carefully fitted and tested; anything that did not fit perfectly was sent back to the factory for alteration. By March 1889, the Eiffel Tower was complete, and on March 31 of that year, Gustave Eiffel celebrated the occasion by a formal opening, limited to government officials and representatives of the press. When the party reached the top (they walked; the elevators were not yet in service), Eiffel hoisted a French flag, with a 25-gun salute fired from below.

Although the formal opening was on March 31, work continued until nine days after the official opening of the Exposition on May 6, when the Eiffel Tower was first opened to the public. Nearly two million visitors visited the Eiffel Tower before the festival's end.

Gustave Eiffel's twenty-year contract for the tower ended in 1909, when ownership reverted to the city of Paris, which originally planned to tear it down. However, the tower was extremely useful for communication, so it was allowed to stand. Eiffel built an apartment on the very top level where he carried out meteorological observations.

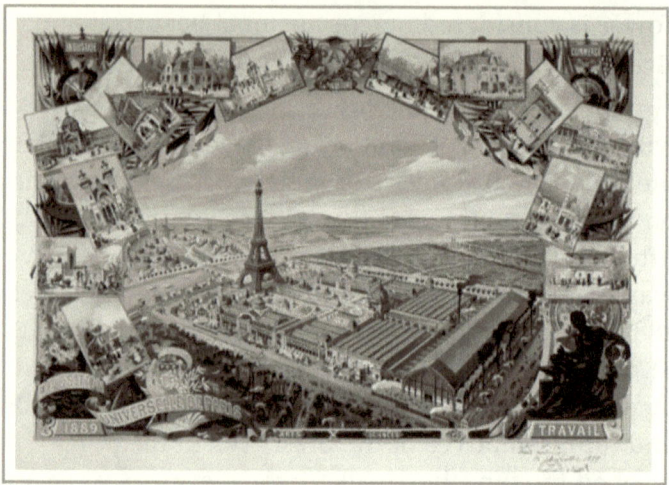

Engraving of the 1889 Exposition Universelle showing the Eiffel Tower as the entrance arch to the festival.

When the Nazis conquered Paris in World War II, the French cut the lift cables so Adolf Hitler would have to climb the steps to the summit. German soldiers did climb the tower to hoist the swastika, but the large flag blew away a few hours later and was replaced with a much smaller one. Hitler didn't climb the tower; when he visited Paris, he stayed on the ground.

In 2002, the tower received its 200 millionth visitor. It is such an icon of Paris that movie critic Roger Ebert once noted that no matter where in Paris a film is set, the Eiffel Tower will be visible in the background.

March 31 Holidays and Celebrations

Bunsen Burner Day (Scientific community, worldwide)

Bunsen Burner Day is an unofficial holiday to celebrate the birth of the inventor of the Bunsen burner, German chemist Robert Wilhelm Eberhard Bunsen (some sources say "von Bunsen.") Interestingly, most official records list Bunsen's birthday as March 30 (he's featured in the March 30 volume of *The Story of a Special Day*), although later sources list March 31 instead. There is agreement on the date of his death, however: August 16, 1899, in Heidelberg, Germany.

César Chávez Day (United States)

César Chávez Day, commemorating the life and work of labor leader César Chávez, is celebrated on March 31 each year through service to the community. In California, Colorado, and Texas, it is an official state holiday. Texas, Arizona, Colorado, Michigan, Nebraska, and New Mexico also recognize the day officially, and César Chávez Day is normally proclaimed by the President of the United States.

Jum il-Ħelsien (Malta)

Jum il-Ħelsien, or Freedom Day, is a national holiday in Malta celebrating the final withdrawal of British troops and the Royal Navy from that nation on March 31, 1979. This marked the first time in hundreds of years that Malta was no longer a military base of a foreign power.

King Nangklao Memorial Day (Thailand)

วันที่ระลึกพระบาทสมเด็จพระนั่งเกล้าเจ้าอยู่หัวฯ (*Wan Thi Raluek Phra Bat Somdet Phra Nangklao Chao Yuhua*) is a national observance in Thailand commemorating the birthday of King Nangklao (พระบาทสมเด็จพระนั่งเกล้า เจ้าอยู่หัว, *Phra Bat Somdet Phra Nangklao Chao Yu Hua*), also known as King Rama III.

King Nangklao (March 31, 1787 — April 2, 1851) was the third King of Siam (former name of Thailand), ruling from 1824 to 1851. He was a successful military leader and was also known for his Buddhist piety. His successor, King Mongkut (Rama IV), is famous in English-speaking countries as the monarch in the book *Anna and the King of Siam*, adapted into the play and film, *The King and I*.

National Clams on the Half Shell Day (United States)

In the United States, almost every day of the year is dedicated to a particular food. Sponsored by manufacturers, retailers, farmers, or simply fans, these days are often proclaimed by the President, Congress, state governors, or mayors.

March 31 is National Clams on the Half Shell Day. Native Americans ate clams regularly and made wampum, shell beads used as money, from the shells of whelks and clams. Early American settlers considered clams to be starvation food, although they were similar to English mussels and cockles, and mostly fed them to pigs. Clambakes only became popular following the American Civil War, and in the late 1800s, Italian and Chinese immigrants opened clam shacks and clam bars serving raw clams, which were cheaper than oysters. Overfishing of clams led to a dramatic drop in supply, from 750,000 bushels in 1976 to fewer than 104,000 a decade later.

Thomas Mundy Peterson Day (New Jersey)

On March 31, 1870, African-American Thomas Mundy Peterson (October 6, 1824 — February 4, 1904) became the first African-American to vote in an election under the newly enacted 15th Amendment to the United States Constitution.

A school custodian and handyman, Peterson was the first African-American in the city of Perth Amboy, New Jersey, to hold elected office (he was a county commissioner), and was the first person of color to serve on a jury in that city. Citizens of Perth Amboy raised $70 (over $1,000 in 2010) to create a gold medallion for Peterson to celebrate his vote. In New Jersey, March 31 is recognized as Thomas Mundy Peterson Day.

Thomas Mundy Peterson wearing the gold medal he was awarded by the citizens of Perth Amboy

Transfer Day (US Virgin Islands)

On March 31, 1917, the Virgin Islands were officially transferred from Denmark to the United States, and the anniversary is celebrated in the US Virgin Islands as Transfer Day.

Christian Feast Days

In *Western Christianity*, saints commemorated on March 31 include Abdas of Susa, Acathius of Melitene, Anesius and companions, Benjamin, and Balbina.

In *Eastern Orthodox Christianity*, it is the commemoration of Righteous Joseph the Fair, Saint Hypatius the Wonderworker, Theophilos the Martyr, Martyrs Menander and Sabinus, Saint Apollonius of the Thebaid, Saint Hypatius, Saint Renovatus, Saint Aldo, Saint Guido, Saint Ivan I, Saint Philaret, and Saint Innocent. (These are celebrated on April 13 by "Old Calendarists;" see page 92.)

Other Holidays (United States unless otherwise noted)

Some holidays are simply made up by individuals, companies, or other organizations, and whether they become widely adopted depends on whether people choose to celebrate them. Here are some opportunities to celebrate on March 31.

March 31 is National "She's Funny That Way" Day, celebrating the humor of women; Terri's Day, marking the anniversary of the death of Terri Schiavo (see "Who Died on March 31"), known for the legal battle over her life support after she was diagnosed as being in a persistent vegetative state; Oranges and Lemons Day; and Tater Day.

The *USS Missouri* in preparation for the Japanese surrender ceremony (see page 25)

What Happened on March 31?

627 – Battle of the Trench

A key event in the early history of Islam, the Battle of the Trench (in Arabic, غزوة الخندق, or *Ghazwah al-Khandaq*) took place after Muhammad and his early followers were expelled from Mecca and took refuge in Medina. Battles took place at Badr and Uhud, in which superior Muslim tactics defeated numerically stronger opponents.

A confederation of forces opposed to Muhammad assembled an army of around 10,000 to attack the Muslim fortifications at Medina. With only 3,000 troops at his disposal, Muhammad dug trenches that rendered the enemy cavalry useless and used diplomatic strategies to undermine the Confederate alliance.

Following the Muslim victory at Medina, Muhammad's political stature grew and Islam became increasingly influential in the region. The battle is chronicled in the 33rd *sura* (chapter) of the Qur'an.

1492 – Edict of Expulsion

On March 31, 1492, Spanish monarchs Ferdinand and Isabella (better known to Americans for their sponsorship of Christopher Columbus) issued the Alhambra Decree that expelled all Jews from their kingdom.

Any Jew who did not convert to Christianity was given four months to leave the country or be subject to death without trial. Estimates of how many Jews left Spain range from 130,000 to 800,000; tens of thousands were killed trying to reach safety. Spanish Jews who converted to Christianity (between 50,000 and 70,000) were persecuted and most were eventualliy forced to leave the country. The Edict of Expulsion was not formally revoked until 1968.

1774 – Boston Port Act

Following the Boston Tea Party, the British Parliament ordered the closing of the Port of Boston by passing the Trade Act of 1774 (Boston Port Act) on March 31, 1774. This became known as one of the "Intolerable Acts," and formed one of the causes of the American Revolution that began the following year.

1906 – NCAA Founded

On March 31, 1906, the Intercollegiate Athletic Association of the United States (IAAUS) was founded to establish uniform standards and regulations for college athletics in the United States.

Impetus for the organization came from two White House conferences led by President Theodore Roosevelt, followed by a series of meetings among colleges and universities. In 1910, the organization changed its name to the National Collegiate Athletic Association (NCAA), and has grown from an initial membership of 62 colleges and universities to nearly 1,300 today.

1909 – Construction of *RMS Titanic* Begins

In 1908, the ship construction firm of Harland and Wolff received an order from the White Star Line to build three giant ocean-going vessels, *RMS Olympic*, *RMS Titanic*, and *HMHS Britannic*. Later that same year, drawings for the ships were approved. The construction of *RMS Olympic* began on December 16, 1908, and *RMS Titanic* on March 31, 1909. Construction took approximately two years.

Titanic was launched on May 31, 1911, and set out on its first voyage on April 10, 1912, only to sink five days later. *HMHS Britannic* went into service in 1915 as a hospital ship, and hit an underwater mine off Greece and sank in 1916. Of the three ships, *RMS Olympic* had the longest career, staying in service for 24 years, retiring from service in 1935.

RMS Titanic and RMS Olympic under construction, October 1910
(Photo: Robert John Welch)

1930 – Hays Code Adopted

On March 31, 1930, the Motion Pictures Producers and Distributors of America (MPPDA) adopted the Motion Picture Production Code, generally known as the Hays Code for its chief enforcer, Will D. Hays. The Code was adopted in response to increasing public response to risqué films, and greatly restricted motion picture content.

Although a few non-Code films were produced, generally the Code was followed until the late 1950s, and slowly eroded as public opinion changed. The MPPDA, now known as the Motionn Picture Association of American (MPAA), developed a rating system to replace the Code. The MPAA rating system went into effect in 1968, and with modifications has remained in force.

1933 – Civilian Conservation Corps

As part of FDR's New Deal approach to the Great Depression, the Civilian Conservation Corps (CCC) was authorized by Congress on March 31, 1933. The CCC provided unskilled manual labor jobs for the unemployed in the area of conservation and development of natural resources in rural areas.

Over the nine years of the program, approximately three million young men participated in CCC projects, receiving shelter, clothing, food, and $30 per month ($537 in 2013 dollars) — $25 ($447) of which had to be sent home to their families. By 1942, with increasing American involvement in World War II, the need for the program declined and it was discontinued.

CCC workers build a road in Pennsylvania
(Gerald W. Williams Collection)

1949 – Newfoundland Joins Canada

From 1907 to 1949, the former British colony of Newfoundland, consisting of the island of Newfoundland and the North American mainland area of Labrador, was a British Dominion rather than part of Canada. In 1949, through a popular vote, Newfoundland decided to join the Canadian confederation, becoming the tenth province of that country.

1951 – First UNIVAC 1 Computer Sold

UNIVAC (UNIVeral Automatic Computer 1), made by Remington Rand, was the first American computer designed for business and administrative use.

The very first UNIVAC was sold to the United States Census bureau on March 31, 1951. The computer wasn't actually shipped until December because it was the only fully set-up model and was needed for demonstrations, so the first actual installation was the second computer sold, delivered to the Pentagon in June 1952.

The original price of the UNIVAC 1 was $159,000, or about $1.5 million in 2013. It weighed 29,000 pounds and could perform fewer than 2,000 operations per second.

1966 – Luna 10 Launched

On March 31, 1966, the Soviet unmanned spacecraft Luna 10 was launched from the Baikonur Cosmodrome. It entered lunar orbit on April 3, becoming the first artificial satellite of the moon. The battery operated satellite continued to operate until May 30, when radio signals ceased.

1970 – Explorer 1 Reenters the Atmosphere

The first successful United States satellite, Explorer 1, launched on February 1, 1958, following the Soviet launches of Sputnik 1 and Sputnik 2 the previous year. It continued to transmit data until May 23 of that year, but remained in orbit until March 31, 1970, when it reentered Earth's atmosphere after circling the planet more than 58,000 times.

1985 – First WrestleMania

WrestleMania, an annual pay-per-view (PPV) event organized by World Wrestling Entertainment (WWE), had its first showing on March 31, 1985. Over 19,000 fans attended the match at New York's Madison Square Garden, and over a million more watched on closed-circuit television, making it the largest PPV event to that date. The event featured nine professional wrestling matches, with the main event pitting Hulk Hogan and Mr. T against Roddy Piper and Paul Orndorff, with Hogan and Mr. T victorious.

1992 – Last US Battleship Decomissioned

The *USS Missouri* (BB-63) was the last battleship built by the United States. Entering service on June 11, 1944, it fought in the battles of Iwo Jima and Okinawa, served as the site for the surrender of Japan, fought in the Korean War, and (following a modernization) provided fire support during Operation Desert Storm in 1991. It was officially decomissioned on March 31, 1992, and donated to the USS Missouri Memorial Association to become a museum ship at Pearl Harbor, Hawaii.

La Rêveuse, by Pascin

Who Was Born on March 31?

Art

Pascin (March 31, 1885 – June 5, 1930)

Julius Pincas, better known as Pascin and sometimes called the "Prince of Montparnasse," was a painter in the Modernist movement. He is the subject of a chapter in Ernest Hemingway's A Movable Feast, "With Pascin at the Dôme."

Business and Labor

Evan Williams (March 31, 1972 –)

Internet Evan Williams co-founded Twitter and served as CEO of that company.

Eliyahu M. Goldratt (March 31, 1947 – June 11, 2011)

Israeli physicst and management theorist Eliyahu M. Goldratt developed such management tools at the Theory of Constraints and Critical Chain Project Management. His best known work is the 1984 "management novel" The Goal, which models systems management in the area of strategic capacity planning and constraint management.

Liz Claiborne (March 31, 1929 – June 26, 2007)

Fashion designer Liz Claiborne founded the company that bears her name, which became the first company founded by a woman to make the Fortune 500. She was the first female chair and CEO of a Fortune 500 company.

César Chávez (March 31, 1927 – April 23, 1993)

Farm worker, labor leader, and civil rights activist César Chávez co-founded what became the United Farm Workers (UFW) union, becoming a major icon of the Latino community and organized labor. His birthday, Cesar Chavez Day (see page 13), is a state holiday in California, Colorado, and Texas.

César Chávez (Photo: Joel Levine)

Alfred E. Hunt (March 31, 1855 – April 27, 1899)

Metallurgist and industrialist Alfred E. Hunt founded the company that would become Alcoa, the world's largest producer and distributor of aluminum.

Government, Law, and Politics

Al Gore (March 31, 1948 –)

Al Gore, Jr. (next page), was the 45th Vice President of the United States and the Democratic Party nominee for President in 2000, losing the election to George W. Bush despite winning the popular vote. He previously served as a Congressman and Senator from Tennessee.

Following his vice-presidency, Gore became a leading figure in the climate change movement, for which he was a joint winner of the 2007 Nobel Peace Prize.

A documentary about Gore, *An Inconvenient Truth*, won the 2007 Academy Award for Best Documentary, and in the same year he was named a runner-up for *Time* Magazine's Person of the Year. He is the son of Albert Gore, Sr., who also served as Congressman and Senator from Tennessee.

Al Gore

David Eisenhower (March 31, 1948 –)

Grandson of US President Dwight D. Eisenhower
and son-in-law of US President Richard Nixon,
David Eisenhower is the namesake of the
Presidential retreat Camp David. He is known as a
public policy professor and academic. His wedding
to Julie Nixon inspired the writing of the 1969
Creedence Clearwater Revival song "Fortunate Son."

Michael Savage (March 31, 1942 –)

Radio talk show host Michael Savage is a conservative political commentator. Under his birth name, Michael Weiner, he has written books on herbal medicine and homeopathy. In 2009, he was barred from entering the United Kingdom for "seeking to provoke others to serious criminal acts and fostering hatred."

Patrick Leahy (March 31, 1940 –)

Patrick Leahy has served as US Senator from Vermont since 1975, chairing the Senate Judiciary Committee and serving as President *pro tempore* of the Senate, making him third in the Presidential line of succession.

Barney Frank (March 31, 1940 –)

Barney Frank served as a member of the US House of Representatives from Massachusetts from 1981 to 2013.

He was the first member of Congress to voluntarily come out as gay.

Zviad Gamsakhurdia (March 31, 1939 – December 31, 1993)

Dissident, scientist, and writer Zviad Gamsakhurdia (ზვიად გამსახურდია) was the first democratically elected president of Georgia following the breakup of the Soviet Union. He escaped Georgia following a coup d'état against him in 1991 and died in exile.

John H. Wood, Jr. (March 31, 1916 – May 29, 1979)

US District Court Judge John H. Wood, Jr., nicknamed "Maximum John" for handing down lengthy sentences to drug dealers, became the first federal judge assassinated in the 20th century. Charles Harrelson (father of actor Woody Harrelson) was convicted of the murder, which was ordered by drug dealer Jamiel Chagra.

Prince Henry, Duke of Gloucester (March 31, 1900 – June 10, 1974)

Third son of British monarch George V and Queen Mary, Prince Henry was appointed potential regent for his niece Princess Elizabeth (later Queen Elizabeth II) after his brother George VI ascended the throne, in case George VI should die while his niece was still a minor. He was a soldier most of his life, and served as the 11th Governor-General of Australia.

Military

Shōichi Yokoi (March 31, 1915 – September 22, 1997)

Shōichi Yokoi (横井 庄), a sergeant in the Imperial Japanese Army during World War II, was one of the last three Japanese soldiers to be found after the end of the war in 1945. He spent 28 years in the jungles of Guam before being discovered on January 24, 1972.

Music and Dance

Willem Duyn (March 13, 1937 – December 4, 2004)

Dutch singer Willem Duyn was half of the pop duo Mouth & MacNeal, whose 1972 hit "How Do You Do" was #1 throughout Europe and #8 on the US pop charts.

Herb Alpert (March 13, 1935 –)

Herb Alpert achieved five number one albums, eight Grammy Awards, fourteen platinum albums, and fifteen gold albums as a recording artist with Herb Alpert & the Tijuana Brass, and co-founded the label A&M Records.

John D. Loudermilk (March 13, 1934 –)

Singer-songwriter John D. Loudermilk is best known for songs he wrote for other performers and groups such as "Indian Reservation" (Paul Revere and the Raiders), "Ebony Eyes" (The Everly Brothers), "I'll Never Tell" (Roy Orbison), "Turn Me On" (Norah Jones), and "You Call It Joggin' (I Call It Runnin' Around)" (Mose Allison), and recorded a number of songs in the late 1950s and early 1960s under the stage name Johnny Dee.

Anita Carter (March 13, 1933 – July 29, 1999)

Anita Carter was a member of country music's The Carter Sisters, which were featured on the *Grand Ole Opry* and *The Johnny Cash Show*. Her solo hits includ "Down the Trail of Achin' Hearts," "Blue Bird Island," and "I Got You."

Lefty Frizzell (March 13, 1928 – July 19, 1975)

Country music singer-songwriter Lefty Frizell is a member of the Country Music Hall of Fame and received a Grammy Hall of Fame Award for his long career. His well known songs include "Long Black Veil," "Saginaw, Michigan," and "If You've Got the Money I've Got the Time."

Shoshana Damari (March 13, 1923 – February 14, 2006)

Yemenite-Israeli singer Shoshana Damari (שושנה דמארי) was known as the "Queen of Hebrew Music.

Etta Baker (March 13, 1913 – September 23, 2006)

Piedmont blues guitarist and singer Etta Baker received the North Carolina Folk Heritage Award and the NEA National Heritage Fellowship and recorded numerous albums.

Red Norvo (March 31, 1908 – April 6, 1999)

Jazz vibrophonist Red Norvo, known as "Mr. Swing," played with Benny Goodman, Woody Herman, Billie Holiday, Dinah Shore, and Frank Sinatra. He appeared in the the 1960 Rat Pack film *Ocean's 11*, backing Dean Martin's "Ain't That a Kick in the Head?"

Red Norvo (Photo: William P. Gottlieb)

Joseph Haydn (March 31, 1732 – May 31, 1809)

Classical composer Joseph Haydn made important contributions to the development of the symphony and string quartet. His famous works include the London Symphonies (which include the Surprise Symphony, No. 94 in G major) and his Cello Concerto. He was friends with Mozart and Beethoven.

Joseph Haydn, by Thomas Hardy

Johann Sebastian Bach (March 31 [O.S. March 21], 1685 – July 28, 1750)

Johann Sebastian Bach (next page) is generally regarded as one of the greatest composers of all time, His more than 1,110 known compositions include such classics as the *Brandenburg Concertos*, the *Mass in B Minor*, and the *Well-Tempered Clavier.* The most important figure of the Baroque period in classical music, Bach was best known in his own lifetime as an organist, and became known for his compositions only after his death.

His family was important in the history of Western music for nearly two centuries. His sons Carl Philipp Emanuel Bach, Johann Christian Bach, Wilhelm Friedemann Bach, and Johann Christoph Friedrich Bach were all composers, and over 50 members of the Bach family were professional musicians and composers. Bach's first cousin Johann Christoph Bach was also a well-known composer; he died on March 31, 1703.

(The satirical P. D. Q. Bach, invented by Peter Schickele, is supposedly a "forgotten" son of Johann Sebastian Bach, the twenty-first of his twenty children.)

For the meaning of "O.S.," see page 92.

Johann Sebastian Bach, by Joseph Wegner

Performing Arts

Jessica Szohr (March 31, 1985 –)

Jessica Szohr is best known for her role as Vanessa Abrams on the television series *Gossip Girl*.

Josh Saviano (March 31, 1976 –)

Child actor Josh Saviano played the best friend of the lead character in the television series *The Wonder Years*. Following his acting career, he became an attorney.

Alejandro Amenábar (March 31, 1972 –)

Director, writer, and composer Alejandro Amenábar won an Academy Award for Best Foreign Language film for 2004's *The Sea Inside,* and has won numerous awards for his Spanish-language films.

Ewan McGregor (March 31, 1971 –)

Ewan McGregor played heroin addict Mark Renton in the 1996 drama *Trainspotting,* Obi-Wan Kenobi in the *Star Wars* prequel trilogy, and Christian in 2001's *Moulin Rouge!*

Craig McCracken (March 31, 1971 –)

Craig McCracken created the animated series *The Powerpuff Girls* and *Foster's Home for Imaginary Friends*.

Kyle Secor (March 31, 1957 –)

Kyle Secor played Detective Tim Bayliss on the crime drama *Homicide: Life on the Street*.

Marc McClure (March 31, 1957 –)

Marc McClure is best known for playing Jimmy Olsen in the 1978 film *Superman* and its sequels.

Vanessa del Rio (March 31, 1952 –)

Pornographic actress Vanessa del Rio appeared in over 100 porn films, and has appeared in music videos and mainstream television shows including a 1996 episode of *NYPD Blue*.

Dermot Morgan (March 31, 1952 – February 28, 1998)

Irish comedian and actor is best known for his title role in the British sitcom *Father Ted*.

Ed Marinaro (March 31, 1950 –)

As an actor, Ed Marinaro is best known for his role as Officer Joe Coffey in the 1980s television drama *Hill Street Blues*. Previously, he played professional football for six seasons and was inducted into the College Football Hall of Fame for setting over 16 NCAA records during his career at Cornell University.

Rhea Perlman (March 31, 1948 –)

Rhea Perlman is best known for her role as barmaid Carla Tortelli on the sitcom *Cheers*, winning four Emmy Awards in that role. She married actor Danny DeVito in 1982.

Gabe Kaplan (March 31, 1945 –)

Gabe Kaplan is best known for his starring role in the 1970s sitcom *Welcome Back, Kotter.*

Christopher Walken (March 31, 1943 –)

Christopher Walken received an Academy Award and a Golden Globe as Best Supporting Actor for 1978's *The Deer Hunter,* along with numerous other awards and nominations. He has appeared in over 100 movies and television shows, with major roles in *A View to a Kill, King of New York, Batman Returns, Pulp Fiction, Sleepy Hollow, True Romance,* and *Catch Me If You Can.*

Christopher Walken (Photo: John Harrison)

Israel Horovitz (March 31, 1939 –)

Israel Horovitz wrote such hit plays as *Line, Park Your Car in Harvard Yard*, and *The Indian Wants the Bronx*, which won the Obie Award for Best Play and helped start the film careers of Al Pacino and John Cazale.

Joel Godard (March 31, 1938 –)

Joel Godard was the announcer for *Late Night with Conan O'Brien* for its entire sixteen year run.

Shirley Jones (March 31, 1934 –)

Singer and actress Shirley Jones is best known for her starring role in the 1970s TV series *The Partridge Family*, and had starring roles in musical films including *Oklahoma!, Carousel*, and *The Music Man*. She received an Academy Award for Best Supporting Actress for her role in 1960's *Elmer Gantry*.

Richard Chamberlain (March 31, 1934 –)

Richard Chamberlain came to fame playing the title role in the 1960s TV series *Dr. Kildare*, and appeared in such miniseries as *Shōgun* and *The Thorn Birds*. He has won three Golden Globe Awards.

Shirley Jones

Nagisa Oshima (March 31, 1932 – January 15, 2013)

Japanese film director and screenwriter Nagisa Oshima (大島 渚) is best known to American audiences for his 1976 film *In the Realm of the Senses* and the 1983 film *Merry Christmas, Mr. Lawrence.*

William Daniels (March 31, 1927 –)

Former Screen Actors Guild president William Daniels had many notable roles, including Dustin Hoffman's father in *The Graduate*, George Feeny in *Boy Meets World*, the voice of KITT in Knight Rider, and Dr. Mark Craig in *St. Elsewhere*, winning two Emmy Awards in the latter role.

Richard Kiley (March 31, 1922 – March 5, 1999)

Stage, television, and film actor Richard Kiley won two Tony Awards, three Emmys, and two Golden Globe Awards. He originated the role of Don Quixote in *Man of La Mancha*, and won two awards for his role in *The Thorn Birds*. He was the narrator for the tour in the book and movie *Jurassic Park,* and for the theme park ride based on the movie.

Lucille Bliss (March 31, 1916 – November 8, 2012)

Voice artist Lucille Bliss was the title character in *Crusader Rabbit*, Smurfette in *The Smurf*s, and the wicked stepsister Anastasia in Walt Disney's *Cinderella.*

Eddie Quillan (March 31, 1907 – July 19, 1990)

American film actor Eddie Quillan began his career as a child actor in vaudeville and silent films, and continued in movie and television roles. He appeared in 1935's *Mutiny on the Bounty*, 1939's *Young Mr. Lincoln*, and 1940's *The Grapes of Wrath*, and in numerous television guest roles.

Victor Varconi (March 31, 1891 – June 6, 1976)

Silent film star Victor Varconi was the first Hungarian actor to make a film in Hollywood, appearing as Pontius Pilate in Cecil B. DeMille's 1927 film *The King of Kings*.

His career suffered during the transition to talkies because of his accent, though he continued to play small parts, primarily as Hispanic characters, and appeared in the Fred Astaire / Ginger Rogers films *Roberta* and *The Story of Vernon and Irene Castle*, and the 1943 film *For Whom the Bell Tolls*.

Science and Mathematics

Carlo Rubbia (March 31, 1934 –)

Italian particle physicist Carlo Rubbia shared the 1984 Nobel Prize in Physics for his work at CERN that led to the discovery of the W and Z intermediate vector bosons.

Sin-Itiro Tomonaga (March 31, 1906 – July 8, 1979)

Japanese physicist Sin-Itiro Tomonago (朝永 振一郎) shared the 1965 Nobel Prize in Physics with Richard Feynman and Julian Schwinger for his work in quantum electrodynamics.

Sir William Lawrence Bragg (March 31, 1890 – July 1, 1971)

Australian-born British physicist Sir William Lawrence Bragg and his father Sir William Henry Bragg shared the 1915 Nobel Prize in Physics for their work in analyzing crystal structures by means of X-rays, making him at the age of 25 the youngest Nobel Laureate to date. The mineral Braggite, the first mineral discovered with the assistance of X-rays, is named for the two Braggs.

René Descartes (March 31, 1596 – February 11, 1650)

Philosopher, mathematician, and writer René Descartes is best known for his statement *"Cogito ergo sum"* ("I think, therefore I am").

He is sometimes called the Father of Modern Philosophy for his influence on subsequent philosophers, and his writings are part of the standard curriculum for the study of Western philosophy.

He is equally known for his work as a mathematician: he developed the Cartesian coordinate system and Cartesian geometry (also known as analytic geometry), making him one of the key figures in the scientific revolution.

René Descartes, by Jan Baptist Weenix

Sports

Pavel Bure (March 31, 1971 –)

Pavel Vladimirovich Bure (Па́вел Влади́мирович Буре́), nicknamed "The Russian Rocket," played for 12 seasons in the National Hockey Leage, and was inducted into the International Ice Hockey Federation Hall of Fame in 2012.

Tom Barrasso (March 31, 1965 –)

Goaltender Tom Barrasso was inducted into the United States Hockey Hall of Fame in 2009.

Gordie Howe (March 31, 1928 –)

First recipient of the National Hockey League Lifetime Achivement Award, Gordie Howe is the only player to have competed in the NHL in five different decades, beginning in the 1940s. A member of the World Hockey Association Hall of Fame, Howe is generally considered to be one of the greatest hockey players of all time.

Jack Johnson (March 31, 1878 – June 10, 1946)

American boxer Jack Johnson, known as the Galveston Giant, was the first African-American world heavyweight boxing champion, defeating Canadian Tommy Burns after the previous white heavyweight champions refused to fight a black man.

At the height of the Jim Crow era, Johnson's victory resulted in substantial animosity and cries for a "Great White Hope" to regain the title. Johnson defeated numerous opponents, including former heavyweight champion James J. Jeffries in a 1910 bout billed as the "Fight of the Century." His victory over Jeffries triggered race riots when police and angry white people attacked celebrating black people; twenty people were killed. A film of the bout was widely banned.

Johnson became a major celebrity, endorsing various products. He married three times, all to white women, a major taboo of the time.

He was arrested twice for violating the Mann Act against "transporting women across state lines for immoral purposes" and was convicted the second time by an all-white jury in the courtroom of future baseball commissioner Kenesaw Mountain Landis, even though the alleged incidents had taken place before the Mann Act became law.

He fled the country and lived abroad for seven years, finally surrendering to Federal authorities. During his incarceration at Leavenworth Penitentiary, Johnson invented a tool to help tighten loosened fastening devices, for which he received US Patent 1,413,121.

Johnson continued to fight until the age of 60. He died in a car crash in North Carolina after angrily leaving a diner that refused to serve him. He was inducted into the Boxing Hall of Fame in 1954.

The play and 1970 film *The Great White Hope* is based on his career, with James Earl Jones playing the character "Jack Jefferson," based on Johnson.

Documentarian Ken Burns produced a two-part documentary about Johnson, *Unforgivable Blackness*.

Jack Johnson

Words

Marge Piercy (March 31, 1936 –)

Marge Piercy is known for her 1987 New York *Times* bestselling historical novel *Gone to Soldier*s. Her other work includes science fiction and poetry.

Judith Rossner (March 31, 1935 – August 9, 2005)

Novelist Judith Rossner is best known for her 1975 novel *Looking for Mr. Goodbar,* made into a 1977 movie of the same name starring Diane Keaton.

John Jakes (March 31, 1932 –)

Writer John Jakes began as a writer of sword and sorcery fantasy fiction, including the *Brak the Barbarian* series, but became famous for his historical novel series *The Kent Family Chronicles* and *North and South,* which became an ABC miniseries.

John Fowles (March 31, 1926 – November 5, 2005)

John Fowles wrote numerous critically acclaimed best-sellers, most famously *The Magus* and *The French Lieutenant's Woman.*

Leo Buscaglia (March 31, 1924 – June 12, 1998)

Author and motivational speaker Leo Buscaglia, often called "Dr. Love," once had five simultaneous books on the New York *Times* Best Sellers list.

His well known books include *Living Loving and Learning*, *Personhood*, and *Bus 9 to Paradise*.

Octavio Paz (March 31, 1914 – April 19, 1998)

Mexican writer, poet, and diplomat Octavio Paz received the Nobel Prize in Literature in 1990. His well known works include *El Laberinto de la Soledad (The Labyrinth of Solitude)*, the poem "Piedra del sol" ("Sunstone"), and *El Arco y la Lira (The Bow and the Lyre)*, along with critical studies and biographies.

He was a member of the Mexican government's diplomatic corps, serving in India, Tokyo, and Switzerland.

William Lederer (March 31, 1912 – December 5, 2009)

William Lederer is best known for his 1958 collaboration with Eugene Burdick, *The Ugly American*, about American diplomats in Southeast Asia who failed to learn the local culture, which became the basis for a 1963 film of the same name starring Marlon Brando.

His 1957 book *Ensign O'Toole and Me* was adapted into a 1962 television series, and he co-wrote the screenplay for the 1965 film *McHale's Navy Joins the Air Force*.

Vardis Fisher (March 31, 1895 – July 9, 1968)

Idaho writer Vardis Fisher is best known for his novels of the Old West, including 1965's *Mountain*

*Ma*n, adapted into the 1972 film *Jeremiah Johnson*. His novel about the Mormons, *Children of God,* won the 1939 Harper Prize in Fiction.

Mary Chesnut (March 31, 1823 – November 22, 1886)

South Carolinian Mary Chesnut kept an extensive Civil War diary, first published after her death. In 1981, historian C. Vann Woodward's annotated edition, *Mary Chesnut's Civil War,* won the Pulitzer Prize for History. Her diary is considered the most important work by a Confederate author.

Nikolai Gogol (March 31 [O.S. March 19], 1809 – March 4 [O. S. February 21], 1852)

Russian writer Nikolai Vasilievich Gogol (Никола́й Васи́льевич Го́голь) (next page) is famous for such works as *The Government Inspector* and *Taras Bulba*. He was a leading figure in the Russian Natural School. (For the meaning of "O. S.," see page 92.)

Edward FitzGerald (March 31, 1809 – June 14, 1883)

English poet Edward FitzGerald is best known for his translation of the Persian work *The Rubaiyat of Omar Khayyam*.

Nikolai Gogol

Andrew Marvell (March 31, 1621 – August 16, 1678)

English poet Andrew Marvell is best known for the frequently quoted "To His Coy Mistress," which begins, "Had we but world enough, and time." Marvell was also a politician allied with Oliver Cromwell who escaped punishment following the restoration of the British monarchy in 1660. A close friend of poet John Milton, he helped rescue Milton from execution as well. He served in the British parliament and as a government official and diplomat.

J. P. Morgan

Who Died on March 31?

Business and Finance

Henry Taub (September 20, 1927 — March 31, 2011)

Henry Taub founded Automatic Payrolls, Inc., which became ADP, the largest computerized payroll and benefits management service in the US.

Frank Perdue (May 9, 1920 — March 31, 2005)

Frank Perdue was president and CEO of Perdue Farms, which became one of the largest chicken-producing companies in the United States, known for its advertising slogan, "It takes a tough man to make a tender chicken."

Prince Georges V. Machabelli (July 23, 1885 — March 31, 1935)

Georgian nobleman and diplomat Prince Georges Vasili Machabelli (გიორგი მაჩაბელი) emigrated to the United States after the 1921 Soviet invasion of Georgia and established a perfume company in the United States.

J. P. Morgan (April 17, 1837 — March 31, 1913)

Financier J. P. Morgan was the leading financial figure of his era, responsible for the formation of such companies as General Electric and the United States Steel Corporation.

He was a major figure in resolving the financial crises of the Panic of 1893 and the Panic of 1907, both of which nearly crippled the American economy. He was scheduled to travel on the ill-fated maiden voyage of the *RMS Titanic*, but cancelled at the last minute.

Government and Military

Raúl Alfonsín (March 12, 1927 — March 31, 2009)

Raúl Alfonsín was the first democratically elected President of Argentina following the years of military rule, serving form 1983 to 1989.

Bella Abzug (July 24, 1920 — March 31, 1998)

Women's movement leader Bella Abzug was a member of the House of Representatives from 1971 to 1977.

She helped found the National Women's Political Caucus and chaired the National Commission on the Observance of International Women's Year in 1975.

She was inducted into the Women's Hall of Fame in Seneca Falls and received numerous other honors.

Bella Abzug (Photo: Warren K. Leffler, US News & World Report)

Mineichi Koga (September 25, 1885 — March 31, 1944)

Imperial Japanese Navy Fleet Admiral Mineichi Koga (古賀 峯) became commander in chief following the death of Admiral Isoroku Yamamoto, and died in a plane crash while overseeing the withdrawal of the Japanese combine fleet from the Philippines during World War II.

John C. Calhoun (March 18, 1782 — March 31, 1850)

South Carolina politician John C. Calhoun was Vice President under both John Quincy Adams and Andrew Jackson, served as Secretary of State and Secretary of War, and was both a senator and representative from South Carolina. He is best remembered today for his active defense of slavery as a "positive good," and is considered a force in the eventual secession of the American South that led to the Civil War.

Music

Mel McDaniel (September 6, 1942 — March 31, 2011)

Country music singer Mel McDaniel had a number of hits in the 1980s, including "Baby's Got Her Blue Jeans On."

Selena (April 16, 1971 — March 31, 1995)

Known as the "Queen of Tejano Music," Selena Quintainilla-Pérez was a top selling Latin artist who won numerous awards, and was the only female artist to have five albums in the US Billboard 200 at the same time. She was murdered at the age of 23 by the former president of her fan club. The 1997 film *Selena*, starring Jennifer Lopez, chronicles her life.

Daguerreotype of John C. Calhoun by Matthew Brady

Mitchell Parish (July 10, 1900 — March 31, 1993)

Lyricist Mitchell Parish is known for such works as "Star Dust," "Stars Fell on Alabama," "Sophisticated Lady," "Moonlight Serenade," and the English lyrics of "Volare." He was inducted into the Songwriters Hall of Fame in 1972.

O'Kelly Isley, Jr. (December 25, 1937 — March 31, 1986)

O'Kelly Isley, Jr., was a founding member of the musical family group The Isley Brothers and co-wrote their hit song "Shout."

Johann Christoph Bach (December 6, 1642 — March 31, 1703)

First cousin once removed to the more famous Johann Sebastian Bach (see "Who Was Born on March 31"), Johann Christoph Bach was in his time considered a composer as important as his cousin, and certain compositions attributed to Johann Sebastian Bach have been subsequently recognized as having been written by Johann Christoph. Johann Christoph's eldest son, Johann Nicolaus Bach, was also a composer.

Performing Arts

Shirley Mills (April 8, 1926 — March 31, 2010)

Actress Shirley Mills appeared in *The Grapes of Wrath* and as the title character in the controversial *Child Bride*, filming a nude scene at the age of 12.

Jules Dassin (December 18, 1911 — March 31, 2008)

American film director Jules Dassin was considered one of the leading postwar filmmakers before being blacklisted for membership in the Communist Party during the 1930s. He moved to France and revitalized his career as a European filmmaker.

Anne Gwynne (December 10, 1918 — March 31, 2003)

Film actress and World War II popular pin-up Anne Gwynne (next page) was known as one of the first "scream queens" for her roles in horror films such as *House of Frankenstein* and *Teenage Monster*. She also appeared in *Flash Gordon Conquers the Universe* and *Dick Tracy Meets Gruesome*, and in the first filmed series for television, *Public Prosecutor*.

Anne Gwynne (left) with Patric Knowles in
The Strange Case of Doctor Rx (1942)

Brandon Lee (February 1, 1965 — March 31, 1993)

Son of martial arts film star Bruce Lee, actor and martial artist Brandon Lee died in an accident while filming *The Crow*.

Jerry Paris (July 25, 1925 — March 31, 1986)

Actor and director Jerry Paris is best remembered for playing the next-door neighbor in the 1960s sitcom *The Dick Van Dyke Show.*

Meena Kumari (August 1, 1932 — March 31, 1972)

Indian film actress Meena Kumari starred in more than ninety films in a 30-year career, and is regarded as one of the most influential Hindi movie actresses of all time.

Public Figures

Terri Schiavo (December 3, 1963 — March 31, 2005

Terri Schiavo became the focus of a legal struggle when she slipped into a persistent vegetative state following a massive heart attack in 1990 and her husband petitioned the courts for the removal of her feeding tube. Fourteen appeals and numerous motions at all levels of Federal and state courts along with active protests from pro-life and disability rights groups resulted in the case being highly publicized. (See "March 31 Holidays" for Terri Schiavo Day.)

Olaudah Equiano (circa 1745 — March 31, 1797)

Olaudah Equiano was enslaved as a child but managed to purchase his freedom, and later worked as a merchant and explorer throughout the New World before settling in the United Kingdom. His autobiography, *The Interesting Narrative of the Life of Olaudah Equiano*, depicting the cruel practices of Virginia slave lord, was influential in the abolitionist movement in England and the passage of the Slave Trade Act of 1807, which abolished the slave trade in the British Empire.

Olaudah Equiano

Science and Medicine

Clifford Shull (September 23, 1915 — March 31, 2001)

Clifford Shull shared the 1994 Nobel Prize in Physics for the development of the neutron scattering technique.

Charles Herbert Best (February 27, 1899 — March 31, 1978)

Medical researcher Charles Herbert Best was one of the co-discoverers of insulin.

Hans Fischer (July 21, 1881 — March 31, 1945)

German organic chemist Hans Fischer won the 1930 Nobel Prize for Chemistry for the synthesis of bilirubin and haemin.

Emil Adolf von Behring (March 15, 1854 — March 31, 1917)

German physiologist Emil Adolf von Behring won the very first Nobel Prize in Physiology or Medicine in 1901 the discovery of diphtheria antitoxin.

Sports

Jesse Owens (September 12, 1913 — March 31, 1980)

African-American track and field athlete Jesse Owens (photo, page 2) won four gold medals at the 1936 Summer Olympics, held in Germany, enraging Adolf Hitler, who planned for the games to demonstrate "Aryan racial superiority." On his return to the United States, he was prohibited from commercializing his fame, and ended up in poverty. In later life he was rediscovered and was appointed a US Goodwill Ambassador.

Ralph DePalma (December 18, 1882 — March 31, 1956)

Italian-American racing champion Ralph DePalma won the 1915 Indianapolis 500 and probably more automobile races than any other driver in history. He is a member of numerous automotive racing halls of fame.

Knute Rockne (March 4, 1888 — March 31, 1931)

Notre Dame football coach Knute Rockne is one of the most famous and most highly regarded coaches in the history of American college football. He popularized the forward pass and turned Notre Dame into a football powerhouse, posting the highest all-time winning percentage of a Divsion I football coach. He died in an airplane crash in 1931.

Knute Rockne football card

Words

Enid Bagnold (October 27, 1889 — March 31, 1981)

British author and playwright Enid Bagnold is best known for her 1935 story *National Velvet*, made into a 1944 film of the same name starring Elizabeth Taylor.

Charlotte Brontë (April 21, 1816 — March 31, 1855)

Charlotte Brontë was the eldest of the three literary Brontë sisters, and wrote the classic novel *Jane Eyre*, originally published under the pen name Currer Bell.

John Donne (1572 — March 31, 1631)

Considered the most important of the metaphysical poets, John Donne is best known for his *Devotions Upon Emergent Occasions*, which consists of a series of meditations about recovering from a serious illness, including the famous *Meditation XVII*, which contains the phrases, "No man is an island" and "Never send to know for whom the bell tolls; it tolls for thee."

Donne was a lawyer and diplomat turned priest who served as Dean of St. Paul's Cathedral in London, and also served as member of Parliament.

John Donne, by Isaac Oliver

März (March), by Hans Thoma

The Month of March

"Up from the sea, the wild north wind is blowing
Under the sky's gray arch;
Smiling I watch the shaken elm boughs, knowing
It is the wind of March."
— *"March," John Greenleaf Whittier*

In ancient Rome, March was the first month of the year. As the first month of spring, in the Mediterranean climate it marked the beginning of the military campaign season. That's why March (*Martius*) is named in honor of Mars, the Roman god of war.

Although the first month of the year was moved back to January sometime during the transition of Rome from a kingdom to a republic (historians differ), March was the first month of the year in Russia until the end of the 15th Century, and is the first month of the year in many other cultures and religions.

In the northern hemisphere, March 1 marks the beginning of meteorological spring. In the southern hemisphere, March is the equivalent of September, making southern hemisphere March the beginning of autumn.

March is one of the seven months that have 31 days in it. March starts on the same day of the week as November every year, and except for leap years starts on the same day as February. March starts on the same day of the week as the previous June except for leap years, and in leap years starts on the same day as the previous September and December.

March in Other Cultures

The month of March has different names in different languages. Some nations use calendars other than the Gregorian, and their months may overlap with November. Still, they often have a word for November itself.

Arabic (Egypt, Sudan, Yemen): مارس (Māris)

Chinese and Japanese: 三月

Croatian: Ožujak

Czech: Březen

Finnish: Maaliskuu (earthy month).

Greek: Μάρτιος

Hebrew: מרץ

Hindi: मार्च

Korean: 3 월에 (3 wol-e)

Old English: Hreþmōnaþ

Polish: Marzec

Russian: март

Slovene: Sušec

Ukrainian: березень (birch tree)

Vietnamese: 腩呬 (tháng ba)

March Superstitions

"Beware the Ides of March (March 15)!"

"March comes in like a lion and goes out like a lamb."

"April borrowed from March three days, and they were ill."

The first three days of March are unlucky "blind days." If rain falls on these days, farmers will have poor harvests.

Children born on Easter Day will be fortunate; children born on Good Friday are doomed to be unlucky.

"If Our Lord falls in Our Lady's lap / England will meet with a great mishap." (If Good Friday or Easter fall on Lady Day, March 25, the Feast of the Annunciation of Our Lady, national misfortune will befall.)

Clothes washed on Good Friday will never come clean.

Children should not climb trees on Good Friday.

Bread baked on Good Friday will never go moldy; eggs laid on Good Friday will no spoil.

Marriages that take place during Lent will have trouble.

"Married when March winds shrill and roar / Your home will be on a distant shore."

Good days to be married in March are March 3, 5, 13, 20, and 23. Which day? "Monday for wealth, Tuesday for health, Wednesday the best day of all, Thursday for losses, Friday for crosses, Saturday for no luck at all."

March Symbols

Birthstone Aquamarine and bloodstone, both representing courage.

Aquamarine

Birth Flowers Daffodils

Daffodil

March Events

Honorary Months

Presidents, Congresses, and nations around the world issue proclamations recognizing particular months to honor certain causes. These events generally fall in March. (All US unless otherwise noted.)

- American Red Cross Month
- Child Life Month
- Fire Prevention Month (The Philippines)
- Irish-American Heritage Month
- Colorectal Cancer Awareness Month
- National Caffeine Awareness Month
- National Celery Month
- National Cheerleading Safety Month
- National Flour Month
- National Frozen Food Month
- National Noodle Month
- National Nutrition Month
- National Peanut Month
- National Sauce Month

- Women's History Month (celebrated in Canada during October)

Women's Suffrage Demonstration 1917

"March Madness" (United States)

The NCAA Men's Division I Basketball Championship, popularly known as "March Madness" or the "Big Dance," is a single-elimination tournament to establish the champion college basketball team.

Moveable and Multi-Day Events

Some events take place over a specific week or time period. Start and finish dates may vary from year to year. Some events occur on different days each year (such as "fourth Saturday of a month").

Birkat Hachama (ברכת החמה) (Judaism)

According to the Talmud, the Sun was created at the vernal equinox position at the beginning of the Jewish month of Nisan, established by tradition as March 25 on the Julian calendar.

The Birkat Hachama, "Blessing of the Sun" is recited when the vernal equinox occurs at sundown on a Tuesday, which happens every 28 years. When the Julian calendar gave way to the Gregorian calendar in 1582, the date shifted forward, and continues to shift slowly forward by approximately a day per century.

Birkat Hachama took place on April 8, 2009 (14 Nisan 5769), and will occur next on April 8, 2037 (23 Nisan 5797).

Birkat Hachama at the Western Wall, 2009

Earth Hour (International)

On Earth Hour, held on the last Saturday of March each year, households and business are urged to turn off all non-essential lights for one hour between 8:30pm to 9:30pm on each person's local time. The goal is to raise awareness of the need to take action on climate change.

Meat-Free Week (Australia)

Meat-Free Week, the last week in March, promotes vegetarianism.

National Cleaning Week (US)

National Cleaning Week, the last week of March, reminds us to start our spring cleaning.

Pediatric Nurse Practitioner Week (US)

Pediatric Nurse Practitioner Week is celebrated during the last week of March.

Seward's Day (Alaska)

Seward's Day, celebrated on the last Monday in March, commemorates the signing of the Alaska Purchase Treaty on March 30, 1867.

Easter Season

La crucifixion by El Greco

The Christian holiday of Easter in Western
Christianity is held on the first Sunday after the
Paschal Full Moon following the March equinox,
which is officially set at March 21 by church
reckoning.

Easter itself can therefore occur as early as March
22 and as late as April 25, but occurs most often in
April. In Eastern Christianity, which uses the Julian
calendar, Easter occurs between April 4 and May 8.
This also sets the date for the various events that
lead up to Easter, most importantly the events of
Holy Week.

Passion Sunday

The fifth Sunday of the Christian season of Lent is
known as Passion Sunday in various Protestant
denominations and by some traditionalist Catholics.
Sometimes, the sixth Sunday of Lent is referred to as
Passion Sunday, but it is more commonly known as
Palm Sunday.

Passion Sunday starts the two-week Passiontide,
which ends on Holy Saturday, the day before Easter,
commemorating the day that Jesus's body was laid
in the tomb. The fifth Sunday of Lent can occur as
early as March 8 (though the next time it will be that
early is in 2285 CE), and as late as April 11.

Palm Sunday

The moveable feast of Palm Sunday commemorates
the triumphant entry of Jesus into Jerusalem, an
event mentioned in all four gospels.

In many Christian churches, palm leaves are distributed to the worshippers. The earliest date for Palm Sunday is March 15, and the latest is April 18.

Maundy Thursday

The Thursday before Easter is Maundy Thursday, when the Last Supper took place. Because of its relation to Easter, the earliest day it can occur is March 19, and the latest it can occur is April 22.

Good Friday

Good Friday, observed during Holy Week on the Friday preceding Easter Sunday, commemorates the crucifixion of Jesus and his death at Calvary. Because of its relation to Easter, the earliest day it can occur is March 20, and the latest it can occur is April 23.

Holy Saturday

Sometimes called Easter Eve or Black Saturday, Holy Saturday commemorates the day in which Jesus's body lay in the tomb. Some mistakenly refer to this day as "Easter Saturday," but that properly describes the Saturday following Easter, the last day of Easter Week. The earliest it can occur is March 21, and the latest it can occur is April 24.

Easter

Easter celebrates the resurrection of Jesus Christ on the third day after his crucifixion.

In the liturgical calendar, Easter follows the season of Lent, and begins the period known as Eastertide, which ends on Pentecost Sunday.

Easter is observed religiously in a morning service. In the U.S., it's also common to decorate Easter eggs and make Easter baskets of eggs and candy, often with the Easter bunny as a symbol. The White House traditionally hosts an egg hunt, and many communities have Easter parades.

Easter customs around the world include bonfires (Cyprus, western Sweden), men spanking women with a ceremonial whip (Czech Republic and Slovakia), egg fighting (Bulgaria), cross-country skiing and reading murder mysteries (Norway), and children dressed as witches collecting candy door-to-door (other Nordic countries).

Easter Eggs

Easter Monday

In some Roman Catholic and Eastern Orthodox cultures, the Monday after Easter is celebrated as a holiday. It is also known as Egg Nyte, featuring egg rolling competitions and dousing other people with water that had been blessed with holy water the previous day at mass. Easter Monday is also celebrated as Family Day in South Africa. In Guyana, people fly kites that were made on Holy Saturday. In Portugal, it is known as the Anjo (Ivy) Festival, in which people picnic in the countryside.

Śmigus-Dyngus (Poland, Hungary, Czech Republic, Slovakia)

The Monday after Easter in Poland and in the Polish diaspora is known as *Śmigus-Dyngus*, or simply Dyngus Day in the US. Boys throw water over girls they like and spank them with pussy willows. Girls avoid getting wet by giving boys "ransoms" of painted eggs.

Easter Week (Western Christianity), Bright Week (Eastern Christianity)

The period from Easter Sunday to the following Saturday is known as Easter Week. In both Western and Eastern Christianity (where it's known as Bright Week), the resurrection continues to be celebrated in church services. Easter Tuesday is a public holiday in the Australian state of Tasmania.

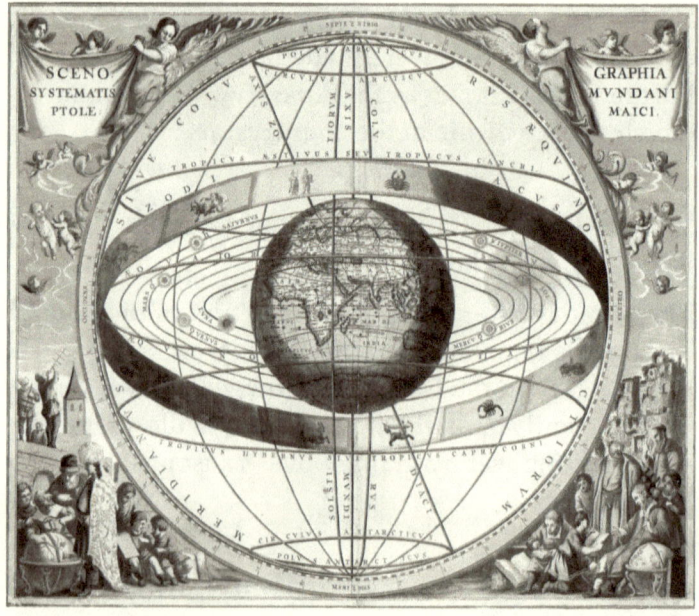

Scenography of the Ptolemaic Cosmography, by Johannes van Loon, based on Andreas Cellarius's *Harmonia Macrocosmica,* 1660

March Zodiac Signs

From the perspective of someone on Earth, the Sun appears to move through the sky throughout the year, along a path astronomers call the *ecliptic plane*. The ecliptic plane is divided into twelve constellations, known as the zodiac, based on traditionally observed patterns of stars. On your birthday, you can't see your constellation, because it's in the daytime sky.

The zodiac was first developed by Babylonian astronomers about 2,500 years ago. Because they were unaware that the Earth wobbles like a spinning top (known as *precession*), they didn't make allowance for the fact that the Sun's path through the zodiac changes over time.

That means there are now two sets of dates for your birth sign. The *tropical dates* are the original Babylonian dates; the *sidereal dates* tell you where the Sun actually appears as it moves along its annual path.

For March 31, the tropical sign is **Aries**, and the sidereal sign is **Pisces.**

Pisces

Tropical February 20 to March 20
Sidereal March 15 to April 14

In the Roman legend of Venus and her son Cupid, they escaped the clutches of Typhon, known as the "father of all monsters," by transforming into fish and tying themselves together with rope. That's why the name Pisces is plural for fish. The constellation appears as a somewhat ragged "V" shape, representing the rope, with the "fish" located at the two rope ends.

In astrology, Pisces is a water sign, compatible with the other water signs Cancer and Scorpio, as well as with the earth signs Taurus, Virgo, and Capricorn. Pisceans are supposed to be imaginative, compassionate, unworldly, secretive, and escapist.

Aries

Tropical March 21 to April 19
Sidereal April 15 to May 15

In Greek mythology, Aries is a ram with golden wings and golden wool who rescued the twins Phrixus and Helle from certain death. Although Helle died in the rescue attempt, the grateful Phrixus sacrificed the ram to Zeus. The golden fleece from the sacrificed ram played a prominent part in the later myth of Jason and the Argonauts.

In astrology, Aries, a fire sign, is compatible with the other fire signs of Gemini, Leo, and Sagittarius, and to a lesser extent with air signs Scorpio and Libra. Arians are supposed to be adventurous, enthusiastic, quick-tempered, and impulsive.

Illustration by Edward Penfield

What Day of the Week is March 31?

On what day of the week does March 31 fall?

Surprisingly, this isn't an easy question. Because the calendar year is 365 days long (366 in leap years), it doesn't divide evenly by the seven days of the week.

Also, the Earth goes around the Sun in about 365-1/4 days, so a calendar tends to drift over time. That's why the same date falls on different weekdays in different years.

This is made even more complicated by a change in calendars that took place in 1582. Our modern calendar has its roots in ancient Rome, in a calendar reform conducted by Julius Caesar. Caesar commissioned mathematicians to attack the problem, and they came up with the idea of leap years, and thus standardized the calendar for centuries to come. This was called the Julian calendar.

Over time, however, the small errors in Caesar's calculation compounded. That's why Pope Gregory XIII commissioned the Gregorian calendar, used in most of the world today. Some countries converted in 1582, when the calendar was first developed; some converted later; other still haven't changed.

Gregorian and Julian aren't the only types of calendars. The Hebrew year, the Islamic year, and many other calendars are used in different parts of the world and among different people.

You can convert Gregorian dates to other calendars, including the Hebrew calendar, the Islamic calendar, and even the Mayan calendar by visiting the Fourmilab Calendar Converter at http://www.fourmilab.ch/documents/calendar/.

Chinese calendar systems are quite complex and have changed several times; a full discussion is far beyond the scope of this book. If you're interested, you can find information here: http://www.hermetic.ch/cal_stud/chinese_cal.htm.

On Names and Dates

Historians use "CE" (Common Era) and "BCE" (Before the Common Era) instead of the more common "AD" (Anno Domini, or Year of Our Lord) and "BC" (Before Christ), reflecting the fact that the year-numbering system established by the Gregorian calendar is used throughout the world in many countries not culturally Christian.

The CE/BCE designation dates back to at least 1708, and has been adopted as a standard by the United Nations and the Universal Postal Union. Because this series of books covers events and people of all nations and cultures, we use the CE/BCE terms.

The abbreviation "O.S." ("Old Style") on some dates refers to the fact that the Russian Empire did not switch from the Julian to the Gregorian calendar at the same time as the rest of Europe, and therefore some figures and events have two dates.

Also, in the Julian calendar in England in the 16th century, the year began on March 25 rather than January 1. To avoid confusion with Gregorian dates, dates between January and March were often written using both years.

People and events whose original names are not in the Western alphabet have their native names (where possible) in the appropriate script shown in parenthesis. If you are using an e-reader to access an electronic version of this book, all characters don't always display on all devices.

A 50-year brass perpetual calendar.

Cartoon by John T. McCutcheon

Copyright, Credit, and Contact

Follow Us

Our blog Dobson's Improbable History (http://improbhistory.blogspot.com) features short articles on events and people associated with each day, and updates several times each week. You can also get a daily "What Happened In History" message and all the latest Timespinner Press news by following us on Facebook at https://www.facebook.com/TimespinnerPress. Our Twitter feed @SidewiseThinker links you to all our News of the Day.

Contact Us

Find an error or a format problem? Want information about the series, about us, or about when the volume for your special day might be available? Please email us at editor@timespinnerpress.com. (We also take requests if your special day isn't yet complete. Please give us at least six weeks' notice if possible.)

Sources

We owe a great debt to Wikipedia, which is our first stop for research. We attempt to make independent confirmation of all important dates and facts through a variety of other sources. Other sources we frequently use include the Library of Congress; "on this day" listings from *Encyclopedia Britannica*, the *New York Times*, and the BBC; *Chase's Calendar of Events;* and, of course, the always essential Google.

All art and photographs are either in the public domain, used under a Creative Commons license, or with a "fair use" justification, and most frequently come from Wikimedia Commons and the Library of Congress Prints and Photographs Division.

Attribution is provided where possible, or as requested by the copyright owner, or when there is particular historical significance, listed below. For information about any particular illustration or photograph, please contact us.

Credits

- The cover photograph "Pont des Invalides et Tour Eiffel," is by Carlos Delgado, and can be found at Wikimedia Commons. It is used here under CC-BY-SA 3.0. It has been cropped for this use.

- The illustration of the month of March used on the back cover and as the frontispiece is from the French Gothic illuminated manuscript *Les Très Riches Heures du duc de Berry* by the Limbourg Brothers, Jean Colombe, and an intermediate painter whose name is lost to history. It is in the public domain because its copyright has expired. It has been cropped and its color and contrast have been adjusted for use in this book.

- The caricature of Gustave Eiffel comparing the Eiffel Tower to the Pyramids originally appeared in *Le Temps*, February 14, 1877, issue. It is in the public domain because its copyright has expired.

- The original blueprint of the Eiffel Tower by engineers Maurice Koechlin and Émile Nouguier was created in 1884. It is in the public domain because its copyright has expired.

- The photograph of Thomas Mundy Peterson is more than 100 years old and is thus in the public domain because its copyright has expired. The original photographer is unknown.

- The photograph of *RMS Olympic* and *RMS Titanic* under construction was taken in October 1910 by Robert John Welch, official photographer for Harland & Wolff, and is in the collection of the Library of Congress Prints and Photographs Division. It is in the public domain because its copyright has expired.

- The photograph of Civilian Conservation Corps workers building a road in Pennsylvania is from the Gerald W. Williams Collection in the Oregon State University library. No known restrictions exist on the use of this photograph. It has been cropped for its use in this book.

- The photograph of the USS Missouri during the Japanese surrender ceremony is in the collection of the US National Archives and Records Administration, and is in the public domain as a work created by the US federal government.

- The painting *La Rêveuse* by Pascin is in the collection of the Museum of Fine Art of Nancy. It is in the public domain because its copyright has expired.

- The 1974 photograph of César Chávez was taken by Joel Levine, and is used here under CC-BY-SA 3.0.

- The official vice presidential portrait photograph of Al Gore is in the public domain as a work created by the US federal government.

- The circa 1947 photograph of Red Norvo was taken by William P. Gottlieb, and is part of the William P. Gottlieb collection of jazz photographs donated to the Library of Congress Prints and Photographs Division. According to the wishes of William P. Gottlieb, the photographs in this collection entered into the public domain on February 16, 2010.

- The 1791 portrait of Joseph Haydn is by Thomas Hardy, and is in the collection of the Royal College of Music's Museum of Instruments. It is in the public domain because its copyright has expired.

- The 1870 engraving of Johann Sebastian Bach is by Joseph Wegner, and is in the collection of the Bibliotheque National de France. It is in the public domain because its copyright has expired.

- The 1933 Goudey Sport Kings football card of Knute Rockne is in the public domain because although it was published with a copyright notice between 1923 and 1963, its copyright was not renewed.

- The portrait of John Donne is by Isaac Oliver and is in the collection of the National Portrait Gallery, London. It is in the public domain because its copyright has expired.

- The painting *März (March)* is from the calendar book *Festkalender* by Hans Thoma. It is in the pubic domain because its copyright has expired.

- The photograph of aquamarine has been released into the public domain.

- The photograph of daffodils is by "Myrabella," and is licensed under CC-BY-SA 3.0.

- The 1917 Women's Suffrage demonstration comes from the Library of Congress, Prints and Photographs Division, LC-USZ62-31799 DLC, and is in the public domain because its copyright has expired.

- The 2009 photograph of Birkat Hachama at the Western Wall is by "Ingo," and is used here under CC-BY-SA 3.0.

- The painting *La Crucifixión* by El Greco is located in the Museo del Prado. It is in the public domain because its copyright has expired.

- The photograph of Czechoslovakian Easter eggs was taken by Jan Kameníček, who has released the image into the public domain.

- The 1906 automobile calendar is by Edward Penfield, and is in the collection of the Library of Congress Prints and Photographs Division. It is in the public domain because its copyright has expired.

- The 50-year perpetual calendar photograph is in the public domain.

- The cartoon by John T. McCutcheon is from his 1905 collection *The Mysterious Stranger and Other Cartoons* by John T. McCutcheon. It is in the public domain because its copyright has expired.

License Description and Terms

Aside from material purely in the public domain, photographs and other material in this book are used under specific licenses permitting free use, usually with an attribution requirement. For full text and terms of these licenses, click or enter the appropriate links below. If you believe there is an error in the copyright status or attribution of any of these images, please email us.

- Creative Commons Attribution 2.0 Generic (CC-BY 2.0): http://creativecommons.org/licenses/by/2.0/deed.en
- Creative Commons Attribution-Share Alike 3.0 Generic (CC-BY-SA 3.0): http://creativecommons.org/licenses/by-sa/3.0/
- Creative Commons Attribution-Share Alike 2.5 Generic (CC-BY-SA 2.5): http://creativecommons.org/licenses/by-sa/2.5/deed.en
- Creative Commons Attribution-Share Alike 2.0 Generic (CC-BY-SA 2.0): http://creativecommons.org/licenses/by/2.0/deed.en
- Creative Commons Attribution-Share Alike 1.0 Generic (CC-BY-SA 1.0): http://creativecommons.org/licenses/by-sa/1.0/deed.en
- CC0 1.0 Universal (CC0 1.0) Public Domain Dedication (CC0 1.0) http://creativecommons.org/publicdomain/zero/1.0/deed.en
- GNU Free Documentation License (GFDL): http://en.wikipedia.org/wiki/Wikipedia:Text_of_the_GNU_Free_Documentation_License

Timespinner
Press